D0347252

EASTBOURNE
IN OLD PHOTOGRAPHS

THE MANOR HOUSE, houses the Towner Art Gallery and Local History Museum. The fine building is a fitting venue for the splendid art exhibitions held there. Dating from 1734 it was formerly the home of the Gilbert family and was bought by the corporation from the bequest of Alderman Towner, who left the sum of £6,000 for the purpose of acquiring an art gallery, together with 20 pictures from his private collection. Local art and photographical societies are particularly well catered for.

EASTBOURNE
IN OLD PHOTOGRAPHS

COLLECTED BY
CECILE WOODFORD

ALAN SUTTON
1989

Alan Sutton Publishing Limited
Gloucester

First published 1989

Copyright © 1989 Cecile Woodford

All rights reserved. No part of this publication may be reproduced, stored in a retrieval system, or transmitted, in any form or by any means, electronic, mechanical, photocopying, recording or otherwise, without the prior permission of the publishers and copyright holder

British Library Cataloguing in Publication Data

Eastbourne in old photographs.
1. East Sussex. Eastbourne, history
I. Woodford, Cecile
942.2'58

ISBN 0-86299-661-9

Typesetting and origination by
Alan Sutton Publishing
Printed in Great Britain by
Dotesios Printers Limited

CONTENTS

EASTBOURNE COAT OF ARMS. *Meliora Sequimur* (We Pursue Better Things).

For Roy

INTRODUCTION

This book could well be an updated version of the 1864 work of the *Gossiping Photographer* by Francis Firth (1822–1898), if only for its free and easy approach to what may have become simply a record of the history of Eastbourne, about which many qualified historians have previously written. Therefore it has been my aim to combine personal memoranda, handed down from my family, with general research and a quest for old pictorial records – all of which makes the project alive and slightly more exciting. Having laid these foundations I will now proceed to offer a little background history of the town.

In 1803 Eastbourne, as we now know it, was a collection of four small hamlets – Medes (*sic*) to the south-west, South Bourn (now the Town Hall area), and later, towards the end of the eighteenth century, Sea Houses by the sea were built, mostly for agriculture and sheep-breeding; East Bourn, contrary to the general belief, was a little way inland. There were several windmills at this time. The presence of troops stationed in the area gave a certain attraction to the town and the Methodists among the soldiers began holding meetings in the Sea Houses. In 1809 the first Wesleyan chapel was built in what is now Grove Road at the cost of £861.

The shape of things to come really dated from 1860 on land largely owned by the Duke of Devonshire of Compton Place and John Davies Gilbert who lived in the attractive Manor House (now the Towner Art Gallery). An elegant, tree-lined resort emerged, graced with mansions, gardens and public buildings. The natural three tiers of promenades from the pier to the Chalk Quarry (now known as

Holywell) were sympathetically developed. Behind Compton Place was a vast expanse of downland called The Links; in 1886 two enthusiastic golfers, just returned from St Andrews, cut a few holes in the turf to see if it was possible to establish a golf course. One of these men, Mr Arthur Mayhew, approached the duke with a suggestion to utilize the land, with the result that the duke offered the land free of charge and became the first president of the now popular golf course.

Parts of the Old Town still retain some of their charm, especially the old church which contains a monument to Henry Lushington, son of the vicar who, in 1754 at the age of 16, embarked for Bengal – later to be killed. Probably the oldest existing cottages in the town are in Borough Lane, opposite the Lambe Inn. 'The Pilgrims', dating from the twelfth century within the environs of an early monastery with Georgian additions, incorporate a wealth of historic interest. They are now carefully maintained and modernized. The old Manor House was built in 1776 by Henry Lushington for his second wife, Mary, the eldest daughter of Nicholas Gilbert and it eventually became the home of the Davies Gilbert family. Robert Adam is reputed to have been responsible for the gracious interior. At an auction it failed to reach the required sum so, when Alderman Towner died and left £6,000 towards building an art gallery, it was decided the money should be put towards the purchase price of £19,000 and the gallery was officially opened in 1923.

In 1861 the population was only 5,778, by 1871 it was 10,342, in 1940 there were 60,000 inhabitants and, by the late 1980s, this figure had grown to nearly 90,000. The first Mayor after Eastbourne was given borough status was Mr G.A. Wallis. The Duke of Devonshire presented the corporation with a chain while Mr C. Davies Gilbert gave a mace. The first railway was built in 1849 on the Gilbert estate. William Cavendish, who became the 7th Duke of Devonshire in 1858, owned two thirds of the parish. He had inherited Compton Place in 1834 and in 1838 began his plans for the development of the town – a town which has grown in elegance and charm, and, in the Victorian and Edwardian eras possessed great character. A little west of the present railway station, Grove Road leads to the Town Hall which was built in 1884 by Birmingham architect, W. Tadman Foulkes. Further along is the Saffrons Ground which has been the scene of many county cricket matches.

Beyond is Compton Place, designed by Colin Campbell in 1726 and built by Arthur Morris of Lewes. Great spectacles have taken place there, especially when Edward VII, as Prince of Wales, favoured the place. King George V and Queen Mary stayed there while recovering from an illness and a plaque on a chalet along the lower parade at Holywell notes the visit – they often rested there. The present Queen and her sister also stayed there with their parents in 1935 and could be seen playing on the sand. They attended morning service at the parish church. On a later occasion they came together, without their parents, as teenagers and attended All Saints Church. The Royal Parade, too, has royal connections. It was opened in 1882 by the Prince of Wales (later Edward VII). Yet another Prince of Wales (later Edward VIII) visited the Fishermen's quarter and the splendid archway the fishermen built and decorated was greatly admired on 30 June 1931.

The Winter Garden, a most elegant structure of iron and glass, was erected in 1876 and has seen many spectacular occasions; from floral exhibitions to skating, which took place for the first time in 1910. The Winter Garden also incorporated the outside rink around the ornate Indian Pavilion, brought to Eastbourne from the Royal Naval Exhibition in 1891.

Eastbourne was a favourite holiday resort for Lewis Carroll who stayed in a house near Terminus Road and always amused his landlady by arriving with his own tin bath and wearing a top hat (the hat was worn at all times – even on the beach). According to a guide of 1871, 'the little hamlet of Medes (sic)' was 'bleak and breezy'. By 1876 this was amended to, 'although at present only an agricultural hamlet, it will probably be known as the Belgravia of East Bourn.' This prediction proved correct. Tiny cottages scattered along tree-lined streets saw the beginning of solid, but graceful houses. Schools for 'young ladies' and 'young gentlemen' flooded the area combined with an exodus of the wealthy from the town. St John's Church, built in 1869, had to be enlarged twice in a few years. In 1890 the fishing fraternity left the chalk hollow, now known as Holywell, and carried on their 'industry' at the East End on Marine Parade before moving lower down. The 'hollow' was later developed into the charming Italian Gardens. The name 'Holywell' has nothing to do with 'holy' as is generally believed, but is a corruption of 'hollow' in Sussex dialect, therefore meaning 'well in the hollow'.

Learning of the gracious development and wealth pouring into the town one could be forgiven for assuming that poverty scarcely existed. Charities abounded, naturally, but the stark truth stared one in the face in the form of children begging, barefoot, in the gutters – even after the conclusion of the First World War. Then they were joined by war veterans on wooden crutches. A soup kitchen opened in Langney Road for 2d. (taking one's own bowl) it supplied the queue who waited patiently at midday. As old age approached the accepted fate was the Union, or Workhouse (now St Mary's Hospital). Couples were parted and lived out their lives in dumb acceptance.

A contemporary writer of the day says that the Church Parade on Sundays 'is a special feature in Eastbourne and, for the most part, consists of well-dressed ladies and gentlemen. The crowd is as dense as similar gatherings at Brighton during the season. Recent arrivals include H.H. Princess d'Averburg and the Duchess of Buccleuch, etc.' It was certainly a favourite resort for the aristocracy and the Maharajah of Baroda chose Queenwood School for his daughters' education. A national newspaper proclaimed Eastbourne 'the healthiest watering place in the kingdom' – certain proof, if proof be needed, that 'great floods have flown from simple sources'.

Beside the Seaside

AN EDWARDIAN SCENE of the middle parade looking towards the Wish Tower. As it was extremely unladylike to allow the sun to tan one's face – every other part was closely covered – sunshades were essential. On the Wish Tower in the distance people were 'enjoying' the sunshine probably to a state of exhaustion. The group in the photograph on the left is most likely the Salvation Army band which played on that site.

TRACES OF THE OLD SEA HOUSES remain on Marine Parade; the Round House was once a horizontal mill and later frequently used for summer holidays by the children of George III. Notes written over 200 years ago were addressed to: Their Royal Highnesses Prince Edward (later the father of Queen Victoria) and Princess Elizabeth and Princess Sophia.

MOUNT PLEASANT near the Round House in 1860. This features in Theodore Hook's book, *Jack Bragg*. The Wish Tower in the distance is a little out of proportion.

Beachy Head, Eastbourne

THIS PICTURE OF BEACHY HEAD must be one of the most popular ones in Britain. Taken in 1906 it shows part of the cliff long since disappeared. The lighthouse on the rocks below was built in 1902. The structure was rendered necessary by the subsidence of the cliff supporting the old lighthouse at Belle Tout and by the light being frequently obscured by mist and fog. No keeper treads the spiral staircase today as it is automatic.

THE FAMOUS SEVEN SISTERS CLIFFS from which the mouth of the River Cuckmere flows. These have been a welcome sight to many a sailor homeward bound. Each has a name; Went Hill Brow, Baily's Hill, Flagstaff Point, Bran Point, Rough Brow, Short Brow and Haven Brow.

1056. EASTBOURNE FROM PIER.

MARINE PARADE from the pier has seen a lot of changes. In the early days during October and November, when the herring season was in full swing, houses in Beach Road adapted by erecting tall chimneys to aid the industry. The Royal Sovereign Lightship saw the laying of lobster and crab pots. Mackerel, plentiful in early summer, often drew large boats as far as the Irish coast. This photo was taken in 1920.

A GROUP OF CHRISTMAS MORNING BATHERS in 1905 at the pier head. This has been an annual event for the best part of the century.

THE GROUP OF CHRISTMAS MORNING BATHERS at the end of the pier evidently brought along their fox-terriers to enjoy the 'dip', in 1905.

ROUGH SEAS AT SPLASH POINT always draw a crowd, even today. Schoolchildren and adults alike derive great excitement from them. At this point, as at Grand Parade, sea bathing was for ladies only at the time this photo was taken.

VIEW FROM THE QUEEN'S HOTEL opposite the pier, looking towards the Wish Tower, c. 1907.

A VIEW OF THE PIER from the Wish Tower in the early part of this century. Mixed bathing was not allowed in Eastbourne before 1871 and residents and visitors took advantage of the Devonshire Baths built in 1866. Although a sedate walk along the Prom' was considered acceptable (dressed in 'Sunday best', of course), rarely did one sit on the beach. The Salvation Army played at various stands on the beach on Sunday evenings and at the pier entrance at the top of Cavendish Place.

A GOOD EXAMPLE OF THE THREE PARADES termed as; The World (the top parade) The Flesh (the middle parade), and The Devil (the bottom parade). According to one's social status the relevant 'walk' was chosen; although the Sunday morning parade did, on occasions, tread the middle parade, the top was their normal one. The bottom was 'reserved' for trippers, children bowling iron hoops, and certain perambulators. Nannies and their charges usually chose the top parade as the middle one was yellow and gritty.

The Carpet Gardens.
Eastbour

THE FAMOUS CARPET GARDENS without which no book of photographs would be complete. Commencing at the pier and continuing to Victoria Place (now Terminus Road) we see them in full summer glory with the visitors of 1910 enjoying the sunshine along the parade. The Burlington Hotel on the left of the photograph offers its guests a fine view of these gardens in all seasons.

A VERY FOOLHARDY YOUNG MAN risks the ever-present danger of crumbling cliffs. On this occasion in 1935 they had already begun to break up. Within a week the scene was very different. In 1909 Mr H.S. Toms commenced excavations at the Belle Tout lighthouse after being given permission by one of Eastbourne's landowners. The site revealed remains of the Bronze Age. Later, in the summers of 1968–69, a rescue operation on the fast disappearing cliffs revealed a circular hut dating from the Middle Stone Age, taking the story back at least 6,000 years.

ONE OF THE MARTELLO TOWERS on the Crumbles in 1934 falling completely apart. Built to defend the coast when under threat of Napoleon's invasion in the eighteenth century. The height was 32 ft, and circumference at the base 132 ft, with walls from 5 to 6 ft thick. The magazine was placed at the bottom, over which were two rooms for the garrison of from 6 to 12 men. The gun was on the top.

THE BEACH FROM THE GRAND PARADE between the pier and the Wish Tower. Not the cleanest part for trippers as boats left their grease; here they plied for hire with or without a boatman. Children paddled and made sand-castles. Leading directly from the railway station it was the first sight of the sea and consequently was the most congested.

THE WISH TOWER, the old Martello Tower No. 73, and one of the continuous line of towers. Known as the 'Wish' it was opened on Whit-Monday 1970 by the Duke of Norfolk. The usual origin of the name is ascribed to a corruption of 'wash', a wet place, or 'wise', an old English word for marsh, an example of which once existed close by.

THE BANDSTAND at Grand Parade in the balmy days prior to the First World War. With military bands playing stirring music and strollers in straw hats, and sunshades to shield the ladies from the 'dangers' of the sun, who could have imagined that in a few short months a war 'to end all wars' was to change everyone's lives? This was a photograph taken in June 1914.

A RARE VIEW of one of Chapman's early charabancs at the pier entrance; his office is on the right of the picture. This primrose-coloured vehicle had, no doubt, just loaded up with passengers for a trip to Wannock Gardens. In 1905 there would have been little to see compared with ten years later. The admittance to the pier was probably 1*d*.

MARINE PARADE, C. 1890, with Sea Houses and the pier in the background.

ON THE PIER IN 1910. People, some with prams, enjoying the sea air and panoramic views. By now Eastbourne was recognised as a 'healthy resort'.

THE PIER SUFFERED TERRIFIC DAMAGE in 1897 when it was broken asunder in a great storm. The sloping way of the present pier indicates the position.

BELLE TOUT LIGHTHOUSE was erected in 1834 by John Fuller MP. The stone is said to have been drawn by ox teams from Maidstone. The low situation of the building is due to the fact that its light was less likely to be obscured in fog. Beneath the old lighthouse are caves excavated by order of Trinity House for the purpose of providing shelter to shipwrecked seamen.

CONSTRUCTING THE EXISTING LIGHTHOUSE – built in 1902. The foundations are embedded in 18 ft of chalk.

A VIEW FROM THE SEA of the pier and Grand Parade, drawn in the very early days of Eastbourne's popularity with visitors.

THE SEA BEACH HOUSE, seen at the end of the row of Sea Houses on the right, shows the charm and grace which was to be the keynote of building for decades to come. Alfred, Lord Tennyson, enjoyed his stay at this particular house to such an extent in 1842, that he paid a return visit in 1845.

A STRANGE KIND OF CAMERA OBSCURA, admission to which cost 2*d*., standing between the Wish Tower and Grand Hotel. In the distance is All Saints Hospital and Beachy Head. The date is probably mid-nineteenth century, but there appear to be few records of it.

THE 'OLD' BANDSTAND, built in 1882, was a small iron and glass construction known as the birdcage. Here it is nearing its swan-song and was replaced by the present stone building in 1935. This scene in 1930 was typical of its most popular years, when Captain Harry Amers' Municipal Band and the East-bourne Military Band conducted by Mr Durrant brought crowds to three per-formances a day.

THE 'NEW' BANDSTAND built in the early 1930s on Grand Parade was a revelation; it had an arena for seating 3,000, and the musicians had protection against the weather. Yet all too soon the Second World War was to disrupt its performances – this time very severely, and with the barbed-wire entanglements and complete neglect, it was a sorry sight compared with the splendid building of a few years earlier.

THIS IS AN UNUSUAL SIGHT at Eastbourne as the town never encouraged the donkey trade. However, in the early 1970s two were allowed at Prince's Park for children's pleasure.

SECTION TWO

Parks and Gardens

A MEMORIAL to those who fell in the First World War was erected in the 1920s on a lawn in Hampden Park close to the road which winds through the park. A very special tree was planted around 1908 said to be the oldest type in the world – in China it was known to grow to 100 feet. It rejoices in the name of *Metasequoia glyptostroibes*. Close by, up to the late 1920s, a cage containing red squirrels – now a sight probably never to be enjoyed again in the countryside – joined the charming rock garden.

THE MANOR HOUSE GARDENS in July 1930.

HAMPDEN PARK at the turn of the century in this autumn scene was undeveloped in certain parts, in fact the railway station was then called Willingdon station, the population being very sparse. In 1901 when this photograph was taken 'The Decoy' belonging to Ratton was purchased by Eastbourne Town Council and from then on the Park, as it was known, began to take shape.

HAMPDEN PARK in 1910 with the wildlife that are still an attraction to young and old. The peace and tranquility around this pond is always restful.

THIS GARDENER'S COTTAGE at Wootton's Gardens, Wannock, stood until the 1920s when it was replaced by the car park which housed all the cars and visitors aboard the charabancs. Rarely did you see a horse-drawn carriage from then on. There is one 'chara' in the photograph, a primrose-coloured vehicle belonging to Mr Chapman. He was a friendly figure who stood on the corner of Seaside Road and Victoria Place (now Terminus Road) and at the pier entrance handing out brightly coloured leaflets of his fleet of coaches.

THESE WELL LAID OUT GARDENS brought visitors from the horse and carriage era onwards to the day they closed in the late 1960s. Rose walks, tropical birds, rare fruits and tiny shops which sold home-made produce fascinated the visitors and teas were reasonably priced even in the early days. A 1s. 6d. tea on the lawn or in a chalet consisted of a loaf of home-made bread, butter, three tiny pots of jam, fruit cake, scones and cream. Entry here was free.

THE OLD MILL GARDENS at Wannock opposite Wootton's Tea Gardens in 1929, also very popular and well-kept, a favourite drive for visitors.

THE JAPANESE GARDENS at the Old Mill Gardens were always greatly admired. Teas were available on the lawns or patios and the entrance fee of 6*d*. was refunded. In late summer especially, the array of flowers was glorious and an object of interest was a water mill said to have been in existence upwards of 250 years.

The Model Village, Wannock Gardens.

THE MODEL VILLAGE at Wootton's Tea Gardens, Wannock. This lovely model, famous in the 1930s and 40s, later moved to the Redoubt and was greatly admired by visitors.

Colleges and Schools

QUEENWOOD SCHOOL (1906–1940) in Darley Road, Meads. Until the school finally settled in Eastbourne it had a very chequered life. Founded in Caen, Normandy, in 1862 by Mrs Ogier Ward, it later moved several times. It was evacuated in 1940.

PUPILS AND STAFF at Queenwood School in 1896. Staff in centre row (right to left): Mlle Pauline Thibault, Miss Harriet Ward, Mrs G.W. Lawrence, Miss Margaret Lawrence, Fräulein von Detten.

THE HISTORY OF QUEENWOOD SCHOOL, *Many Years – Many Girls* was launched at the Cumberland Hotel in October 1967. Written by Dorothea Petrie Carew, a pupil from before the First World War; the occasion was attended by a number of old girls together with many local dignitaries. This photograph shows two guests, Sonia Woodford and Cecile Woodford obviously enjoying the book.

EASTBOURNE COLLEGE started its life in the second half of the nineteenth century. To commemorate its centenary in 1967 Vincent M. Allom, who spent his working life of 37 years on the staff of the college, wrote *Ex Oriente Salus*, a history which takes the reader through all the changing scenes of life at the college, from the days when the building lay on the edge of cornfields to the midst of a well-known coastal resort. It is Doctor Charles Christopher Hayman to whom we owe the beginning of this famous school. Professor Frederick Soddy, Sir Hugh Casson and Wing-Commander R.P. Beaumont OBE were among the best-remembered old boys.

ST BEDE'S SCHOOL, Meads, on 14 July 1919. This is one of the few remaining schools in the area. Boys of many nationalities have passed through – two Russian boys and a Romanian are included in this photograph. Sir John Ellerman is seated in the fourth row from the back, second to the end.

THIS VERY SMART GROUP OF BOYS belongs to the Eastbourne Municipal Secondary School (later the Grammar School) in St Anne's Road. They were chosen as ball-boys for the Tennis Week at Devonshire Park in 1922. The Headmaster, Mr Blackburn, is in the centre wearing a trilby hat.

BERESFORD HOUSE SCHOOL group of 1927. Founded in 1902 the school stands at the foot of the green hills of Sussex. It is one of the few in Eastbourne which have survived out of some 365 at the turn of the century. Back row: Mary Rouse, Helen Forder, Ailsa Jack, Phyllis Bessant, Marguerite Hoyle (later a Mayoress of Eastbourne), Nancy Parker, Mabel Beech, Angel Lloyd, Marian Cooper. Second row: Florence Leslie-Smith, Barbara Hunter, Isabel Lynn, Pamela Bolt, Betty Cato, Sheila Selfe, Margaret Jessopp, Mary Whiteley, Gwen Wakefield, Barbara Bradshaw, Joan Hunter, Joan Salmon, Barbara Gillies, Erica Randell, Helen Wise, Eileen Porter, Emma Walker-Douglas, Hilda Gartsise, Mary Gerlach. Third row: Betty Martin (later Mayoress of Eastbourne), Betty Simmons, Joan Long, Agnes Chater, Irene Thomas-Colman, Phyllis Wiseman, Vivienne Bridgeman, Mary Thorpe, Nellie Lovely, Doreen Barber, Norah Howden, Frances Cooper, Janet Parker, Barbara Cato, Sheilagh King, Joan Bridgeman, Muriel Lloyd, Betty Hudson. Fourth row: Eileen Gray, Laura Jessopp, Noreen Beech, Miss Foster, Miss O'Connor, Miss Evelyn Hilton (Deputy Head), Miss Agnes Speakman (Headmistress), Miss Walford, Miss Williams, Miss Graham, Matron, Celia Wise, Norma Blagrove. Front row: Rosemary Beattie, Kathleen Hedley, Rita Corneijo, Ruby Marchant, Pearl Hudson, Norah Gatty, Margaret Lawson, Kathleen Phillips, Monica Lee, Phyllis Thomas, Brenda Lee, Jean Neidermayer, Joan Scott, Margaret Rutherford, Iris Marchant, Catherine Lawson, Heather Prichard, Eileen Bobby.

MORDEN LADIES' SCHOOL in 1923 – a typical Dame school, founded in Greenwich in the early twentieth century. Later Miss Louisa and Miss Margaret Green moved to Enys Road. The entire school in 1923 accommodated up to 20 pupils. Back row: Eileen Miller, Dorothy Killick, Araxie Adalian, Dora Fowle, Irene Thomas-Colman, Joan Lloyd, Eileen Brown. Front row: Kathleen Birchfield, Joyce Stredwick, Gwennyth Meager, Muriel Etheridge, Kathleen Leach, Joan Pockney. The two boys are: Yervant Adalian and Victor Smith.

CHILDREN OF THE HIGH SCHOOL PREPARATORY DIVISION in 1949. The stretch of fields beyond was shortly to be built on and the High School eventually handed over its building to the Cavendish School in 1978.

A FEARSOME LOOK at some of the boys as Pirates in 1950 at St Mary's School in Old Town. Christopher Squires on the extreme left appears to be a girl as does the 'pirate' fourth from the left – maybe they were captured in a skirmish.

A CLASS AT DOWNSMEAD SCHOOL in Upperton Road in 1953 is visited by the Mayor of Eastbourne. Mr Wilson, the Headmaster, is on the right.

AN ANNUAL EVENT AT ST BEDE'S shows the boys' gymnastic display before admiring relatives and friends. The school building in the background is a perfect example of the architecture of which the town is so proud, and which townsfolk are fighting to preserve. This picture was taken in 1954.

WILLOWFIELD HIGHER GRADE SCHOOL in 1920–21. Uniforms were introduced a few years later. Back row: Rita Billingham, Dorothy Beaton, Bessie Glenny, Jessie Dyer, Rose Seymore, -?-. Second row: May Neal, Winnie Miles, Winnie Cooper, K. Barton, Dora Wyatt, Ivy Parris, Doris Lindberg, -?-, -?-. Third row: Gwen Searle, Ethel Smith, Phoebe Smith, Rose Smith, Vera Meadows, -?-, Irene Brown, Marjorie Green, Edith Fry. Front row: Olive Rayner, Doris Hatch, Phyllis Sayers, Doris Bruce, Ivy Wootton, Maisie Baker, Elsie Dawes, Winnie Saunders.

THIS GROUP OF PUPILS at Colville House School in 1953 was among those who remained in the town throughout the war. It was one of the smaller boarding schools; the joint headmistresses were Miss Dunster and Miss Carlisle, sitting fifth and sixth from the left, second row.

ST BEDE'S SCHOOL, Duke's Drive, Meads, flies the Union Jack for the Coronation of Queen Elizabeth II.

THE REAR OF ST BEDE'S standing on the edge of the cliffs at the foot of Beachy Head.

Recreation

A GROUP PHOTOGRAPH TAKEN IN THE DEVONSHIRE PARK GROUNDS of some of the cast of *Carousel*, a 1965 production by the Eastbourne Operatic and Dramatic Society. Mr Clarence Long is second from the left in the top row and Mr Geoff Fuggle fourth from the left in the top row.

HIKING WAS NO EASY TASK in 1910. Wearing high heels and large hats with dresses sweeping the ground, these four ladies took to the road on bank holidays and followed the coast road from Eastbourne to Brighton. At the back are Maude and Mary Dennis (daughters of the landlord of the Wheatsheaf Inn) and below them: Rose Bonner (from the Terminus Hotel in Eastbourne) with Jessie Huggett.

THIS HAPPY GROUP OF CHILDREN is enjoying a Saturday afternoon in 1923, in Bluebell Woods at Abbotts Wood near Eastbourne, in the charge of Mr Barker who is seated at the bottom of the photograph. From left to right: Joan Pockney, Joan Barker, Mollie Martin, Irene Thomas-Colman, Ray Savage, Marjorie Bellamy.

THREE YOUNG MEN camping at Birling Gap in the summer of 1930.

CYCLISTS OF EASTBOURNE followed a very healthy pursuit at weekends. This group was taken in 1932.

A GROUP OF GIRLS who formed the Mary Mills School of Dancing cabaret. This photograph shows them at the Devonshire Park Conservative dance in December 1929. Top line from the left: Phyllis Hookham, Agnes Chater, Esme Harvey, -?-, -?-, Joyce Sayers, Jose Chapman, Audrey Turton. Second line from left: Vera Harvey, Irene Thomas-Colman, Joan Guy, Nancy Smith, Sylvia Warren, Joan Thwaites. Third line from left: Heather Swaddling, Joan Sutton, Daphne Weatherstone, Joan Linnell, Yvonne Linnell, Eileen Hepton, Jean McClintock, Eva Kidder.

HIKERS FROM EASTBOURNE beside the old cross at Alfriston in 1935. Unfortunately the cross was demolished by a motor vehicle in the 1950s and a new one had to be erected. The group from left to right are: -?-, Cyril Veness, ? Veness, George Nunn, John Fowle, Reg Kitchen, -?-. Front: Steve Dines.

TWO CHILDREN proudly showing off their snowman in December 1947. It was a very hard winter and a coal shortage caused much hardship.

THE CRICKET TEAM of Louis G. Ford in 1935; this was disbanded when war broke out.

RESTING ON THE HILL-CREST above East Dean. This view of surrounding countryside is one of the loveliest in this part of Sussex. The field below has been the scene of many a cricket match. The village green is very popular, with the Tiger Inn and old flint-walled houses; a winding road leads to Birling Gap and in 1932, when this photo was taken, traffic was less and walking was a popular pastime.

THE COUNTRYSIDE HAS BEEN CONSIDERABLY DEVELOPED 30 years later and this photo, taken in exactly the same spot in 1962 unfortunately shows the shape of things to come. There is still a lot of downland free from buildings – but who can tell, say in another 30 years?

BOYS OF EASTBOURNE SCRIPTURE UNION waiting on the station for their annual camping holiday, 25 August 1956.

THIS HIKING PARTY in 1937 was grateful for a rest on the beach at Birling Gap, beneath the Seven Sisters. From the front: Richard Woodford, Maisie Goodman, George Nunn, Connie Livings, Arthur Foster and Leslie Leach.

GROUP PHOTO OF THE CAST OF *CAROUSEL*, 1965, by the Eastbourne Operatic and Dramatic Society at the Congress Theatre. Mr Clarence Long, the well-known tenor, is at the end of the bottom row; beside him is Miss Jean Saul.

CLARENCE LONG in the Vagabond King in 1961. Mr Long, the head choirboy in Winchester Cathedral in his youth, joined the Eastbourne Operatic and Dramatic Society in 1959 – his first show being *Bless the Bride*. He played in 25 productions.

GEORGE SQUIRES, left, and his wife Ethel, with two friends enjoying camping at Norman's Bay in July 1958.

CAMPING AT NORMAN'S BAY in 1961. From left: Barry Garcia, Neil Squires, Terry Garcia, Rosalind Garcia, George Squires.

A LONE CAMPER on cliffs at Birling Gap in 1960 frying his breakfast. During the night a severe storm had swept away most of the tents and survivors had packed up and left. This small tent had stood the test well, not to mention the young camper.

EASTBOURNE POLICE ORCHESTRA in 1927. Top row: Miss E. Collins, Mrs N. Crighton, PC Cunningham. Bottom row: PC Watch, PC Comber, PS Jackson, PC Iliff, PS Curtis, PC Bailey, PC Crighton.

Events and Celebrations

CORONATION TABLEAU by the boys of St Bede's in June 1953.

A PAIR OF SKATERS on Eastbourne pier rink at the Christmas Carnival in 1905. Mary Dennis and Wally Hamblin were a popular couple during that skating era – it was to be another 25 years before the craze came around again, then it was the Devonshire Park that laid down a rock maple floor and saw several seasons of skating.

THE ANNUAL BOXING DAY MEET of the Foxhounds on Beachy Head in 1912. This event took place until the Second World War.

THE BOXING DAY MEET at Beachy Head in 1933. The southdown drivers on the right have brought coach loads of visitors to this well-known event.

THE MANOR HOUSE GARDENS was the venue for these young dancers from the Eastbourne School of Dancing which was held in the Towner Art Gallery. It was a delightful contribution towards the town's Victory Week celebrations in 1946, after the end of the Second World War, entitled 'Dance of the Allies'.

VISITORS FROM HOLLAND at the Manor House dancing display during Eastbourne's Victory Week, 8 June 1946.

A PROCESSION OF CHILDREN IN FANCY DRESS stretching along Victoria Drive and heading for the party at St Elisabeth's Church on 2 June 1953 to celebrate the Coronation.

THE FIRST PRIZE WINNER at the fancy dress party was a very topical dress. The Everest expedition 'climber' on Coronation Day wore a placard on his back cut from the headlines of the *Daily Express* of that morning '– All this – And Everest too!'

LEYLAND LION NO. 12, 1939. Decorated splendidly for the 1953 Coronation. Both the small models on the top and the bus itself still exist.

Ships

THE *BERYL TOLLEMACHE* answering a distress call. This lifeboat was presented and launched in 1949 by Sir Lyonel and Lady Tollemache, joining scores of lifeboats that have rescued shipwrecked vessels. The men's complete dedication and heroic deeds have saved thousands upon thousands of lives. The first permanent lifeboat museum opened in 1937 in a boathouse built by public subscription 40 years earlier in memory of an actor, William Terriss.

THE *SOVEREIGN* LIGHTSHIP was popular for trippers aboard the *Brighton Belle* from which this photograph was taken in the 1920s. Years later it still saw pleasure boats making the round trip until a new structure (still manned) replaced it in the early 1960s.

THE LIFEBOAT LAUNCHING is always good for an interesting snapshot. This photograph was taken in 1929.

SEPTEMBER 1955 saw the *Germania* crippled off the beach.

ENJOYING THE SEA AIR aboard the *Waverley*, one of the paddle boats that started from the pier in pre-war days. This photograph was taken in 1923.

ALL ABOARD THE *SKYLARK*. A crowded beach beside the pier, c. 1912.

THE *EASTFIELD* was stranded on the rocks at Beachy Head in 1909. A German submarine which was being towed broke loose in a storm and was washed ashore alongside the wreck.

BEACHED *EASTFIELD* AND SUBMARINE in 1909.

SS BARNHILL BOMBED IN THE CHANNEL and beached at Langney Point. It was on fire for four days in 1940.

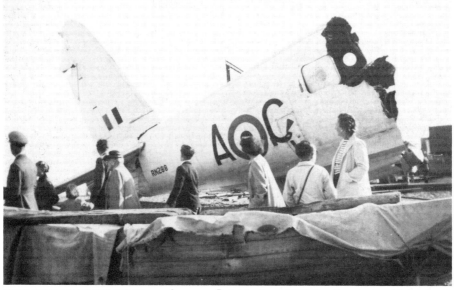

AFTER CRASHING ON THE BEACH near Langney Point in June 1955 the *Sunderland* flying boat later broke up.

SECTION SEVEN

People and their Connections

THE DOG HOUSE at Hankham, home of Eastbourne's Member of Parliament, is a sixteenth-century, grade two listed building. Mr Ian Gow TD, has lived there since 1972. At one time it stood isolated along a deeply rutted track. In winter with snow piled high it was often impassable. A story goes that for many years, on a date when children were imprisoned in the village school because of the deep snow, a light always showed in the window of the old house, but no one knew who lit it.

A DRIVER AWAITING INSPECTION in 1914 outside the Carlisle Mews (later Carlisle Garage) in Langney Road. The proprietor, Henry Thomas-Colman, personally inspected each driver and carriage. The YMCA can just be seen on the right of the picture, which housed the Blue Boys of the First World War.

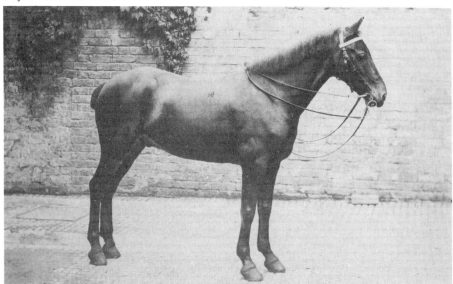

'NOBBY', the last horse to leave Carlisle Mews in Langney Road. After 1917 it was known as Carlisle Garage. The Motor Car Act of 1903 limited the speed to 20 mph – even so, the days of peaceful travel were over. Great clouds of dust smothered the countryside and the strange new attire worn by motorists replaced the smart clothing of horse riders. Few of this new species understood about mechanics and breakdowns were a common sight.

THE PROPRIETOR, Henry Thomas-Colman, and his wife Mary in 1914.

CAROLINE THOMAS-COLMAN, mother of the proprietor, played a large part in entertaining the Blue Boys from the YMCA by giving them a home from home feeling, albeit ration restricted. The large kitchen always had a cosy welcome with its rag rugs on the stone floor, red plush table-cloth, and warmth from the kitchen range. A loaf or two and ginger cookies were usually baking. Her young grandson showed his magic lantern slides.

CAROLINE THOMAS-COLMAN, at the age of 86, enjoying the sea breeze on Eastbourne beach in 1923.

IN THE MID-TWENTIES Harold Humphries Van Tromp left Wolverhampton Hospital where he was a surgeon and settled in Eastbourne. He was a fine Shakespearian actor, a playwright and journalist. He was, in fact, a man of many qualifications and joined the local paper as writer of the leader column, 'Church and Churchman', 'Drama', and 'Books and Bookmen'.

THIS PHOTOGRAPH OF THE RED LION INN at Willingdon shows it in the 1920s with the landlord, Dick Gurr, and his daughter in the doorway; it was built between 1906 and 1908. Wish Hill upon which it stands was the main Eastbourne to London Road. In 1787 G.S. Chambers noted in his book *Old East Bourn* 'some very small cottages appear almost underground' – those 'small cottages' are there today.

ALTHOUGH MODERNIZED, THE RED LION of the 1970s still retains an old world atmosphere.

ANNE PRODGER, photographed in 1860, who lived in one of those 'small cottages'. Of her five children Alfred met an untimely death by falling off a hay wagon on to the prongs of a pitchfork outside the Red Lion, William became coachman at Compton Place to the Duke of Devonshire, and Julia married the landlord of the Wheatsheaf Inn. The church register contains the family names for generations.

BARTEL GEORGE MARTIN, son of Martin the tailor of Willingdon. This photograph was taken in India in 1910 while serving with the 17th/21st Lancers. On several occasions he met the Viceroy, the Marquis of Willingdon, who had firm ties with the village during the years the family had occupied Ratton Manor. Bartel Martin returned home in due course to marry the 'girl next door', namely Adelaide Dennis, daughter of the landlord of the Wheatsheaf Inn.

County Borough of Eastbourne

At a Meeting of the Council of the said County Borough held on Monday the Third day of September 1945,

Present:—

The Worshipful the Mayor (Alderman Miss Alice Hudson, J.P.) in the Chair

Mr. Alderman Martin (Deputy Mayor) and 26 Members of the Council

It was moved by the Mayor, seconded by Mr. Councillor Dingle, M.B.E. and Unanimously Resolved:—

(1) That in pursuance of Sub-section 2 of Section 259 of the Local Government Act 1933, the Council do hereby confer on

The Right Honourable Winston Leonard Spencer Churchill, C.H., M.P.

the Honorary Freedom of the County Borough of Eastbourne and do admit him as an Honorary Freeman of the said County Borough

A COPY OF THE TITLE PAGE from the Album presented to Winston Churchill when he received the Freedom of Eastbourne at the Dorchester Hotel, London, on Thursday 22 April 1946. The Mayor of Eastbourne, Councillor Randolph Richards, made the presentation.

LORD WILLINGDON, Viceroy of India, Governor of Madras, Governor of Canada and a personal friend of King George V was known simply as 'the Squire' to the villagers of Willingdon. Born in 1866 and died in 1941 he endeared himself to everyone during his life at Ratton Manor. Educated at Eton he excelled in cricket playing for the Sussex XI and was a member of the MCC at Lords. He became Warden of the Cinque Ports, from 1937–1941.

LADY WILLINGDON took a tremendous delight in her flower gardens while living at Ratton Manor. Two events of note took place during the years there – the Flower Show and Tenants' Banquet; the former took place in a meadow below the Manor called 'the Coombe', and the latter in the Manor itself. Treading a well-trodden path to the church of St Mary the Virgin in the village, she would lead her staff on Sunday mornings. Should the weather be bad they would arrive in carriages. It was a sad day in November 1918 when the estate was sold by public auction.

CAPTAIN HARRY AMERS (RIGHT) AND SIR EDWARD ELGAR. Captain Amers was Musical Director for the Municipal Band between the wars. The Winter Garden was a much frequented venue on Wednesday nights when he arranged his 'popular' concerts, for the price of 6d. per seat. His Saturday night orchestral concerts were also well attended. During the summer seasons the band played in the 'old' bandstand on Grand Parade.

SECTION EIGHT

Transport

THE 'SUNNY SOUTH SPECIAL', (through train between Manchester and Eastbourne) about to commence its return journey north headed by D.E. Marsh-designed Class T2 4-4-2 tank locomotive No. 196 in 1909.

THE RAILWAY STATION in the days of the old London, Brighton and South Coast Railway. A guide was issued to aid tourists of requisites needed in case of possible breakdowns. 'Carry a flat Portmanteau – not too heavy to carry necessities. Two flannel shirts, two pairs of flannel trousers, two pairs of easy walking shoes NOT very new. A black bag to hold clothes for a night or two. Leather leggings. Strong umbrella. Salt and pepper mixed. Chloroform for toothache. Diarrhoea mixture. Cold-in-the-head mixture. Always keep at least half-a-pint of brandy handy. Blue Dust spectacles.' What, I wonder, would be the equivalent today?

R.J. BILLINGTON'S Class E4 0-6-2T locomotive No. 469 *Beachy Head*, not far from its celebrated namesake, when waiting on an Eastbourne siding in 1909. Of this versatile class of tank engines, 70 were built in the 1890s and they were employed throughout the LBSCR region.

ANOTHER FAMOUS STEAM ENGINE to bear the town's name is 'Schools' Class No. 914 *Eastbourne*, shown here in Southern Railway livery. Designed by Chief Mechanical Engineer R.E.L. Maunsell, a total of 40 were built before 1935 – all named after public schools in Southern England. They were the most powerful 4-4-0 locomotives in Europe and gave sterling service until steam operation ceased on the Southern Region.

STATION PARADE alongside the railway with a few shops and a rank for horse-cabs at the turn of the century.

LOCOMOTIVE ENGINEER William Stroudley's most celebrated express engines were the Gladstones and 36 were built by the London, Brighton and South Coast Railway between 1882 and 1891. No. 183 *Eastbourne* is shown at the Eastbourne terminus in 1902.

THIS STRANGE-LOOKING COMPOSITE VEHICLE is Steam Rail Car No. 1, built for the LBSCR in 1905 for working local services on the line between Eastbourne and St Leonards.

ANOTHER VIEW OF STEAM RAIL CAR NO. 1 approaching Eastbourne Station c. 1908. These self-propelled passenger coaches were not entirely successful and the service reverted to conventional locomotive hauled trains a few years later. The unusual rail vehicle ended its days in Trinidad, British West Indies.

MR HORACE HOLMAN who worked as a journeyman with the railway for 50 years.

A RENAULT, WITH ITS PROUD OWNER in 1924.

A STUDEBAKER model from around 1926. The open-top cars blew away the cobwebs (if you didn't mind inhaling the exhaust fumes *en route*), but when it rained the driver got a real soaking while tackling the portable windows and fixing the hood. The party here were all set for a picnic on the Hide, near Hailsham. They were the Chapman family, owners of the Royal Parade Garage in Cambridge Road.

AUSTIN 12, 1924 model along a quiet country lane.

A DRIVE OUT in a new 1927 Austin 12.

THE ANNUAL CHILDREN'S OUTING at St Elisabeth's Church in Victoria Drive. Ann Barton is probably checking that they are all aboard. The two children beside the coach are Richard Wood and Avril Langridge.

THIS LITTLE GIRL obviously thought it safer to sit on the bumper than beside a rather erratic driver of this 1925 Morris Cowley in 1929. They say a magpie flying past is an ill omen; one just happened to do so earlier and the driver, in following its flight, ended up in the ditch upside-down . . . happily, all escaped injury.

THIS TRAMWAY ran from Royal Parade to the Crumbles from 1954 and continued for about 15 years carrying passengers, chiefly holiday visitors, during the summer season. Although in 1903 Eastbourne became the first British municipal motor omnibus operator, at no time has the town been served by tramways. However, Mr Claude W. Lane constructed a 2 ft gauge line running along the Crumbles, operated by 6 reduced-scale tramcars built in the workshops of Modern Electric Tramways Limited.

EASTBOURNE CLAIMS THE DISTINCTION of being the first municipality in the world to inaugurate a motor omnibus service. Here is one of the first 14-seater, 12/16 hp, Milnes-Daimlers in operation in 1903. Wages were then 5*d*. an hour, and the average working week was 60 hours.

A 1904 MILNES-DAIMLER, one of the first double-deckers, photographed in Ocklynge. There was usually a scramble to sit beside the driver – often a rather greasy spot and not, at this stage, popular with ladies in their flowing dresses!

A DOUBLE-DECKER MILNES-DAIMLER introduced in 1906. This type remained in service until 1919.

A 1916 LEYLAND 'B' CHASSIS supporting a 1914 body; the result of war-time requisitioning. The smartly turned-out staff pose proudly in 1920. This photograph was taken on Royal Parade *en route* for the foot of Beachy Head.

A 1948 LEYLAND PD2 NO. 27 undergoing the tilt test at the factory. The inclination of 36 degrees looks very precarious.

THE 'WHITE KNIGHT' AT THE PIER. New in 1938 and converted to an open top in the 1950s. Many will remember the famous four – the 'White Princess', the 'White Rabbit', the 'White Queen', and the 'White Knight'. The one hour ride was very popular with visitors.

A 1938 AEC REGENT AT EASTBOURNE RAILWAY STATION in 1947. Public transport was in great demand during the austere immediate post-war years.

MAINTENANCE WORKSHOP in Churchdale Road. Staff working on pre-war Leyland Titans c. 1948.

ANOTHER BUSY WORKSHOP SCENE during the 1940s.

MR GEORGE RAE (left) electrician for many years working on Leyland TD 2 Titan No. 78. Four of these pre-war vehicles were converted to open-top in the early 1950s and proved very popular on sea-front routes.

TAXI RANK AT THE STATION. Obviously it was an important occasion for the Union Jack to be displayed. As it was 1913 there appear to be a considerable number of motor cars lined up when one realises that horse traffic was still very much greater at that period.

SECTION NINE

Churches

ST ANNE'S CHURCH in Upperton was once a building of fine architecture – unfortunately it received a direct hit by a bomb in the Second World War.

6732. St. Mary's Church, Eastbourne,

ST MARY'S PARISH CHURCH dates from the twelfth century replacing a Saxon church, probably a wooden structure. It has a low tower and a fine peal of bells recast in 1818. On the south side of the chancel is a brass to Canon Pitman (died 1893) vicar for 62 years. Here again tales are told of smuggling activities and connections with the Lambe Inn close by.

THE PRESENT QUEEN AND PRINCESS MARGARET at St Mary's Church entrance where they attended morning service with their parents, then Duke and Duchess of York, in March 1936.

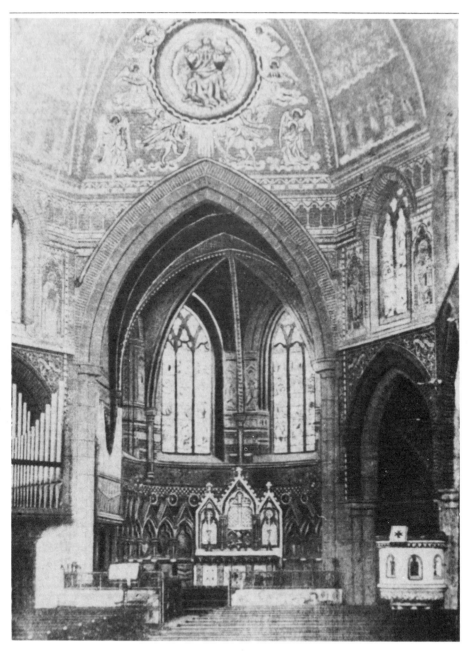

ST SAVIOUR'S CHURCH in South Street is a fine building, especially the interior with its mosaic representing the parables lining the walls. The font, designed by G.E. Street, is of Montezuma onyx, something of a rarity. The spire is 176 ft high, certainly the loftiest of the town. It was erected in 1867 and is one of the more modern churches in Eastbourne.

Trinity Church,
Eastbourne

TRINITY CHURCH in Victorian days. A wide space backed by trees was a favourite place for people to sit on the wooden benches provided, away from the not-so-noisy horse-drawn traffic, on the road beside which elegant houses were built.

THE PARISH CHURCH, WILLINGDON   D17753

THE CHURCH OF ST MARY lies beneath Combe Hill in Willingdon. It has stood there for some 700 years with relics of the Romans, Saxons and Normans in its walls. Until 1939 there were five bells, cast in 1732 – a sixth bell was added in 1939.

SECTION TEN

Streets

A VIEW FROM ST MARY'S PARISH CHURCH looking along Church Street to the High Street in 1909. The Lambe Inn on the left was the place of the arrival and departure of the London coach. At one time fairs took place in the churchyard until a statute of 1286 ordered that neither fairs nor markets should be held on holy ground. The fairs then moved to the roadway. Sheep-fairs were held beside the old Court House amidst cornfields – it was not uncommon to find 12,000 sheep being auctioned at one fair.

OCKLYNGE ROAD looking towards Crown Street c. 1910. This part of the Old Town no longer has its rustic, antiquated cottages – developers have seen to that. The 'old uns' remember though, and the dedicated fought long and hard to save the Star Brewery (see on the right) from having its ancient tower demolished.

SOUTH STREET in the days of crinolines and gentlemen on horseback. The New Hotel (later the New Inn) has changed little over the years. Queries have arisen, from time to time, as to why the Railway Inn nearby is so called. At one time it was planned to have the railway station there and, as the railway arrived in 1849, it is a good supposition as South Street was the most important road in the lower part of Eastbourne.

VIEW FROM ST SAVIOURS CHURCH STEEPLE during its erection in 1861. The streets are Hardwick Road and Blackwater Road. The lawn on the right of the curved road is now Devonshire Park.

TERMINUS ROAD with ladies in crinolines busily shopping and chatting. On the right, Seaside Road winds round and to the left is Trinity Trees.

Victoria Place,
Eastbourne.

THIS SCENE OF THE TOP OF VICTORIA PLACE, or Terminus Road as it is now called, shows a good example of life in 1855 when things were less crowded.

TERMINUS ROAD IN THE EDWARDIAN ERA. Not a very noticeable change, although women's dresses would have altered somewhat; the full skirts would have given way to more slender styles, often with a 'bustle'. The length proved a hazard, however, as they dragged along the rough, muddy streets for which Sussex was renowned.

DEVONSHIRE PLACE IN ALL ITS GLORY with an avenue of trees. Thanks to sympathetic handling it is still a fine road with wide grass verges and colourful flower beds. This was the scene in 1870.

THIS PHOTOGRAPH taken in 1875 is another example of the main Terminus Road. The approach to the town as seen in 1875 was such that its developers could be justly proud. Terminus Road was soon to grow into a busy thoroughfare with commercial ventures and the motor car replacing the horse traffic.

IN MEMORIAL SQUARE stood Princess Alice's Memorial Tree in 1890.

TERMINUS ROAD IN EDWARDIAN DAYS was but one of the splendid tree-lined streets. In Victorian times the town was centred around the railway station and the east end of the seafront. This district was known as the new town to distinguish it from the old town which had begun some centuries before and was situated nearly two miles inland.

SUSSEX GARDENS IN TERMINUS ROAD c. 1900 which later saw shops such as Boots the Chemists, Woolworths etc. rise up, however, the gardens above were retained – not being visible most residents are unaware that they existed.

TERMINUS ROAD showing Boots, Pring's and the London and South Western Bank. Horse carriages still dominated the transport scene in this photograph, c. 1912.

VICTORIA PLACE (now the sea end of Terminus Road) was, in 1910, not the busy shopping centre you see today. Large houses on the left-hand side boasted well-kept gardens and were mostly run by single families. One, owned by a Judge Jeffries, (not the notorious person) hated cats and placed a notice to the effect that any cat found on his land would be shot.

THE ROYAL MARINE HOTEL (later to become the Metropole) on Royal Parade in 1915. A birdcage bandstand stood on the beach here and a concert party, mainly to encourage local talent, played at weekends. An open-top bus is seen on its way to the foot of Beachy Head.

A CHARMING SUMMERTIME VIEW of Ratton coach-houses in 1960. Once on the estate of the Marquis of Willingdon, later Viceroy of India, they are said to be visited by a headless monk on moonlight nights . . . .

SNOWBOUND. The same scene in a Christmas card setting. The author and her dog are knee deep in snow in the winter of 1967 when Eastbourne came to a halt on Friday 8 December. It was well into the New Year before traffic began to move again.

A YOUNG MOTOR CYCLIST decides to leave his journey until the hill at Babylon Way, Ratton, is a bit clearer. This was in February 1963, the snow that had started at Christmas remained deep and treacherous for almost three months.

ONCE AGAIN THE SNOW PROVIDED PRETTY PICTURES but remained for weeks in 1965. Vehicles were abandoned in the outlying districts, although better prepared this time, the main A22 was cleared. Residents in Ratton had to collect their milk from the main road, where the floats parked.

A SCENE SHOWING THE STEEP HILL AT BABYLON WAY in Ratton which was impassable during the heavy snowbound winter of 1967.

SECTION ELEVEN

Shops

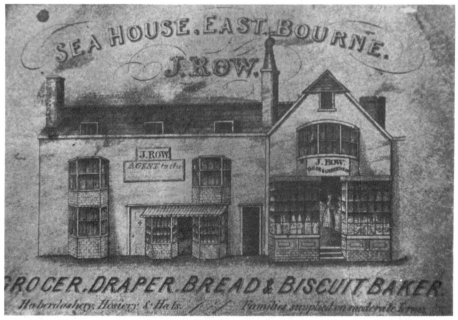

THIS LITTLE SHOP appears to be the local 'supermarket' in the days of the Sea Houses. Research has shown that it was most probably sited just off the shore in the seaside area. The baker's shop, Ye Olde Bakery, c. 1790, is now owned by Mrs Rosalind Ryder-Smith granddaughter of Sam Ryder-Smith, a name well-known to golfing enthusiasts. During reconstruction an ancient oven was revealed dating from around 1840.

A ROW OF SHOPS in the main shopping centre, c. 1907.

SOUTH STREET is certainly one of the oldest streets in Eastbourne. In 1883 a guide to Sussex watering places said: 'There is one street called South Street. There is one very respectable Wesleyan Chapel'. On the left of the photograph Messrs Haines the Undertakers have been on the same site since 1812 – previously a theatre stood behind it. Joseph Carter the town's first constable lived in South Street; his pay was £46 10s. 0d. per annum.

TERRY AND EVENDEN'S SHOP at the corner of South Street and Cornfield Road *c.* 1912.

JAMES S. CHARLWOOD outside his shop which became the first shop front to be opened in Langney Road in 1883.

FREDRICK CHARLWOOD eldest son of James. This photograph was taken around 1920.

ALEC CHARLWOOD second son of James Charlwood. The remarkable thing about this business is that it retains the outward appearance of the original front and still continues to be run by the same family.

TWO CHILDREN, Derrick and Fay Elson, visit the Fairy Grotto and meet Father Christmas in 1952 at Bobby's (now Debenhams) in Terminus Road.

DAVID ELSON in Father Christmas' Fairy Grotto receives his present in 1952. Bobby's in Terminus Road transformed the shop into a wonderland for children.

SECTION TWELVE

Buildings

COMPTON PLACE, home of the Duke of Devonshire has, as previously mentioned, been frequently visited by Royalty – most of all by Edward VII as King and Prince of Wales. The house dates from around 1730 and incorporates a house of 1548. A beautifully situated building viewed from Paradise Drive and the Royal Eastbourne Golf Club – extending across the Links to the Downs.

HARVESTING on the site designated for the Memorial Houses of the Second World War. This was in 1947 and the last time reapers would be cutting the corn. Townsfolk decided to subscribe to this as a tribute for the occupation of disabled men and their families especially as a fine memorial stands in Devonshire Place built after the First World War.

THE GROUP OF LITTLE HOUSES built as a memorial to those soldiers who fell in the Second World War was opened by the Duke of Devonshire in the early 1950s. On the cornfields behind, Ocklynge School was later built.

THE 1914–18 WAR MEMORIAL at the foot of Devonshire Place erected in the 1920s.

THE LAMBE INN, probably the oldest in the county, stands at the top of the High Street in Old Town. It is believed to be the site of the house granted to the rector around the year 1240. The actual date, as confirmed by the present landlord, was that the building took place in 1180 with extensions made during the fifteenth century and, during renovation in 1912, the handsome old beams we see today were revealed. Victorian restorations had completely covered them. Underground passages running between the inn and the church nearby are just another piece of proof of their connection with the smuggling racket.

THE OLD PARSONAGE is a good specimen of a small sixteenth-century manor house. Originally belonging to the Treasurers of Chichester Cathedral, who were rectors of Eastbourne, it came into the hands of the Ecclesiastical Commissioners and was acquired from them by the Duke of Devonshire. In 1912 he generously presented it for parochial purposes, together with a handsome contribution towards the cost of restoration.

THIS PHOTOGRAPH SHOWS THE BEAUTIFUL ARCHITECTURE of the Technical Institute and School of Art in Grove Road. The library and museum were on the lower floor. Silence had to be observed at all times especially in the reading room. Actually children (only allowed in the museum with an adult) were speechless anyway. The life-like tigers and jaguars – not to mention the snakes – were terrifying. Cases contained precious stones and marine treasures.

THE FLORAL HALL in 1909 when the Winter Garden was the centre for the roller skating era. It was a very exciting time and very much an era of more freedom for ladies, especially at the frequent carnivals. The Edwardians certainly made the most of the casting off of gloom and drabness which had prevailed since the death of Prince Albert – the reigning King, Edward VII, led the way to a more relaxed atmosphere.

THE FIRST SCHOOL built in Eastbourne was St Mary's in Old Town in 1814.

THIS IS ANOTHER EXAMPLE OF FINE ARCHITECTURE. The Albion Hotel in the 1920s and other hotels adjoining it along Marine Parade. On the left of the photograph is Caffyn's Garage, one of the first in Eastbourne.

BUILT IN THE EARLY YEARS OF THE LAST CENTURY as part of the long line of coastal defences (of which the Martello Towers are the most famous) the Great Redoubt was part of England's first protection against the French. In 1804 William Pitt's decision to fortify low-lying coastline around south-east England was proved unnecessary, when a year later Nelson's defeat of the French at Trafalgar made the entire system obsolete. However, building continued and the Eastbourne Redoubt was probably completed in around 1812.

SECTION THIRTEEN

Rural Associations

BIRLING GAP showing the old coastguard cottages. People were just beginning to enjoy this rural part of the sea-shore as opposed to the crowded pier area, c. 1919.

THE GILBERT ARMS (Squirrel Inn) once the Hartfield farmhouse, in 1870.

THE POST OFFICE in 1865 on the road leading down from the Lambe Inn in Old Town. It joined the row of cluttered little cottages owned by Benjamin Saunders, a well-known figure in his old blue smuggler's cap and clay pipe. Postmaster George Cook who died in 1857 was 28 years in office. Old Ben, as he freely admitted, was closely connected with the 'gentlemen' who rode the 'darks' — certainly he made an unaccountable amount of money and owned a lot of property in the district.

A SHORT CUT from East Dean village used by campers to Birling Gap in the 1920s and 1930s.

THE OLD GRANARY attached to Susan's farmhouse. It was demolished in October 1898.

SUSAN'S FARMHOUSE around the turn of the century.

EASTBOURNE FROM VICARS MILL 1785, (copy from a drawing by S.H. Grimm in the British Museum).

THE EASTBOURNE VESTRY ROOM erected 1851, demolished in 1902 to make way for the Technical Institute building which, in turn, was destroyed by enemy action in 1943. The entrance to the Sheep Wash pond which was supplied by the Bourne stream is shown behind the boy with a cart.

OCKLYNGE WINDMILL in 1900. This stood on an isolated spot surrounded by farmland and fields of poppies – a truly rural scene. Beyond, the downs were clearly visible and not a house was to be seen in the new built-up area of Victoria Drive where various crescents were built between the wars.

WISH FARM once stood around the area of Carlisle Road and College Road. This picture shows the farm in 1870.

THE MILL, POLEGATE.   D 1347A

POLEGATE TOWER MILL, a popular subject for artists, once again has its fine display of applewood machinery in near-original working order. Saved from demolition by the miller, Mr Albert Ovenden, who allowed the Eastbourne and District Preservation Society (now the Civic Society) to purchase the property for £1,000. It was opened by His Grace the Duke of Devonshire in July 1967. The mill was built in 1817 by Joseph Seymore.

CHALK FARM HOTEL in Cooper's Hill, Willingdon, has a long history dating back to its days as a working farm when, in 1856, a John Paxton was a tenant-farmer of Mr Freeman-Thomas (later Lord Willingdon) of Ratton. The 900 acres were ploughed by oxen; the famous wooden Sussex plough being made by a wheelwright in the village. It was later taken over by a Thomas Cooper (hence the name Cooper's Hill) who organized a Bonfire Night celebration for the villagers, besides other events, when fancy-dress parades circled around the flower bed seen on this photograph.

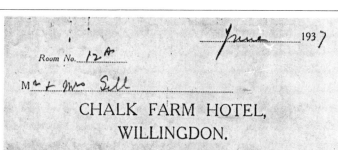

Room No. 12ᴬ

Mᵣ + Mᵣˢ Sill

CHALK FARM HOTEL,
WILLINGDON.

June 1937	20ᵗ	21ˢᵗ	22ⁿᵈ	23ʳᵈ	24ᵗ	25ᵗ	26ᵗ	Total £	s	d
En Pension ...	1/4/-	1/4/-	1/4/-	1/4/-	1/4/-	1/4/-	1/4/-	8	8	—
Apartments ...										
Breakfast ...										
Luncheon ...										
Afternoon Tea										
Morning Tea ...	1/-	1/-	1/-	1/-	1/-	1/-	1/-	7	—	
Dinner ...										
Attendance ...										
Laundry ...										
Paid Out ...										
Telephone ...										
Fires ...										
Minerals ...										
Garage ...										
Cigarettes ...										
Papers ...	2ᵈ	1ᵈ	1ᵈ	1ᵈ	1ᵈ	1ᵈ	1ᵈ		8	
Coffee ...										
Milk ...										

No. **1193** July 26 1938

Mᵣ Sill

Received with thanks for

CHALK FAR

Signed

£8 :15 :8

15 8

AN ACCOUNT FOR A HONEYMOON COUPLE in 1937 who spent a week at Chalk Farm — and returned there again recently. The difference in prices is astounding.

BURNT COTTAGE in Old Town close to the Tally-ho Inn could tell some yarns about the smuggling era. The owner, Mr Harry Spears, was glad his father underwent a fight to keep the old place standing. It was a haven and hoarding place for the smuggling fraternity who frequented that area. For this reason it was burnt down by revenue men. Local residents (being closely connected with the smugglers, no doubt) used their own money to rebuild it in 1830.

THIS CHARMING SCENE OF PEACE AND TRANQUILLITY has long since given way to the modern day hustle and bustle of the A22. In the early 1930s the road cut right through the little village of Willingdon. The church of St Mary the Virgin can be seen, which has stood for some 700 years. As the past is said to be the signpost to the future we will end as we began – *Meliora Sequimur.*

ACKNOWLEDGEMENTS

My warmest thanks are due to the many who have assisted in compiling this book. The Towner Art Gallery and Local History Museum allowed me access to their varied collection of photographs and a special word of thanks must go to Miss Nicky Ingram who gave her time to arranging for reproductions. There are also people who have loaned personal photographs and I am grateful for their help by entrusting them to my care. For his generous help, also, throughout the preparation of the book, my gratitude to Mr F.R. Elson C. Eng. MIEE.

Especially appreciated are the following:

Mr Ian Gow TD MP ● Mr and Mrs G. Squires ● Mr Peter Pyemont (Headmaster of St Bede's School) ● Mr T. Fogg ● Styles Harold Williams ● Mr D. Coleman Mr C.J. Saunders MA (Headmaster of Eastbourne College) ● Messrs Charlwood Miss E. Richards ● Mr C. Long ● Mr H. Thomas-Colman Eastbourne Buses Ltd.